Ode to a *goddess*

poetry & prose

christina antonia

Ode to a goddess Copyright 2020 by
Christina Antonia.

All Rights reserved. This publication may not be used, reproduced, or stored in any system. It may not be transmitted mechanically, electronically, via photocopying or any other means whatsoever without written permission of the publisher.

IBSN: 978-0-6489543-0-9

Editor: Valorie Ruiz
Illustrators: Daniel Domm & Dani Jarrin
Anthotype/ Imagery: Christina Antonia
Book Formatting: Muhammad Faisal Adeel

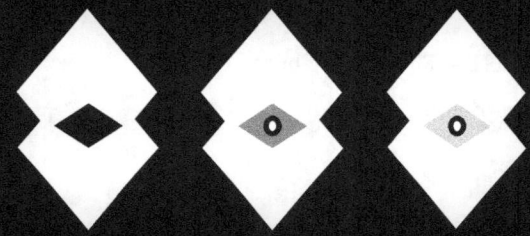

A collective ode:

For all the goddesses finding their way to light

Contents

Acknowledgements	1
Before You Begin	2
I. THE STROPHE - The Black Turn	5
Remembering Begins	6
Snakes	7
Black Licorice	9
No Escape	10
Mammon	12
Oizys And The Foxes	13
Ella, My Love	14
Poseidon P1.	15
Wandering Horus	16
Hypnos	18
Sakura Boy	19
Clotho	20
Snake Venom	21
Antaeus	22
Realisation	23
A Song Dedication	25
Hephaestus	26
Philia	27
I Hoped to Save You	28
Boy Bel Air	30
Eros, From The Stories My Friends Tell	31
Sweet Addict	32
Say No.	33
Libation	34
The Husband Of Aergia	35
Poseidon P2.	36
Ludus	37
Dicky	38
Isfet	39
Mephitis	40
Mania	41
Perses	42
Clapping	43

The Wasps Want The Honey	44

II. THE ANTISTROPHE - To Turn Black — 47

The Year Dodeka	48
Cognition	49
Not a Simple Roar	51
Green	53
Rise The Wolves	54
Under The Influence	55
Concealed	56
Fuckery	57
Ptah in Ruins	59
Escape	60
Mur Mur	61
Dolus	62
Winter	63
Not on Drugs, I Would Never	65
The Only Time Recycling Isn't Okay	66
Melodrama	68
Religion in A Dream	71
Medusa	72
Poltergeist P1.	74
The Death Blame	76
Death Bees	77
Death Noises	78
My Best Friend Never Listened to Me	79
Eat It	80

III. THE EPODE - Said After — 83

Poltergeist P2	84
Shield of Athena	86
Aphrodite	87
Mother Gaea And Her Jasmine	89
Deceive	91
In Your Eyes	93
I Appreciate People When They Go	95
A Black Rose	96
Grand Athena	97
Semo Sancus	98
Prick	99
Daisy Field	100
Tomb	101
You Do Not.	102
The God With an Achilles Heel	103
Vanilla	104

White Linen	105
How to Make Passionfruit	106
Cherry Wine	107
The Ideal Parachute	108
Yiya Christina	110
Drastic Motions	111
Not Just	112
Teething	114
Villains Only Tighten Their Teeth	115
Parfum	116
The Intro	116
The Body	116
The Outro	116
Young Amour Misconception	117
Sleepy Lavender	119
Ode to Esther	121
How to Be a Poet	123
Champagne	124
Neptune's Vanilla Cone	125
Dear Jillian Banks	127
Day of Rest	130
For Your Thoughts	131
Welcome to The End of This Collection	141
One Last Thing	142
About Imagery	143

Acknowledgements

Thank you - to the closest parts of me.

Banks - for speaking in tongues to me during nights I could never sleep. For being the pain and strength that resides in me. My biggest influence and silent guide.

Sharfraz - my solitary and grace, the technical side of me; and my biggest believer in all that I do. You are the person who made all this possible. You heard me cry for hours, then sing. You wiped my eyes and held me, through this whole written piece.

To my Mum Yvonne; Yiya Christina and Aunty Eleni - you've grown me up with open hearts and minds. You've taught me all that I know, and you are the goddesses that brought me to light.

To my cousin, but more of a sister, Emma - for being the gentle voice that keeps me young. Thank you for allowing me to inspire you/ and for even inspiring me.

To all my extended friends and family that contribute to my writing processes, you have made a part of history that will be a part of my life for ever.

And to the man up stairs, who listened to every prayer that I whispered at night.

I love you all, from the deepest parts of me.

christina antonia

Before you begin

For those who hold my book in your hands, I ask one thing of you. I ask you read this with an open mind.

A mind that is aware of the growing frustrations of being young, navigating through human connection and a world I still do not understand. I had an idea of the world— but I couldn't be sure. The three chapter/phases of this book define the 3 vessels of my life so far. There is some coarse language in some areas to express frustrations— that I hope you can remain humble towards. I wanted to make sure that every fragment of me that has ever been built up can finally be put to rest.

The three Chapters build up to an Ode—

The Strophe, The Antistrophe and The Epode. These three partings assisted with communicating my experience of teen hood— and all the emotional turns and growth. To begin with a turn (Strophe), to then enter the pain twice as hard (Antistrophe), and finish with an aftermath of change (The Epode).

Odes are lyrical — or an ode is an expression of gratitude or infatuation towards something.. To me, emotional writings are lyrical within themselves.

I can try my best to make this book anything other than an ode to growth, but still it remains exactly that. Each phase truly happened. Each poem connects to an event, a thought, or a person. It is every part of me that I have ever needed to vent about— in one place.

Goddess, is an important idealism.
It comes from my Greek and Egyptian heritage -
But mostly the song "Goddess" by Banks.
It is the pillar of this book.
It is what kept me standing, writing, positive throughout this process - as well as my 22 years of living so far.

Ode to a Goddess is an ode to the parts of myself that took time, love, and care, to accept and move on from. Still, in reading this, I hope you can find your own emotional poltergeists— find yourself within my pages.

christina antonia

I. THE STROPHE
The black turn

Oh **goddess**, you —
  have formed but you have taken a turn.

You're now experiencing
the deep blue —
the strike, the influence between two.

You've found the deepest parts of you,
and learnt to finally express.

But some expressions, lead to
bloodshed.

Remembering Begins

with vibrations
of all the memories of adrenaline
running through my body, like a violin
shaking me, and flowing
through a river of melancholy

I love it
*I loved it

Snakes

Sometimes you return,
up my neck,
leak into my ears -
consume my brain
fear upon fear.
Sometimes it's more than one of you.
All because you all took a part of me with you.
Now you always find your way back.
You find a hole to nest in,
A white rabbit to fest with.
All the sparkling parts that I am left with—
you eat up.
With a sense,
with a visual,
with a song
and a taste
that ties back to
back then.

christina antonia

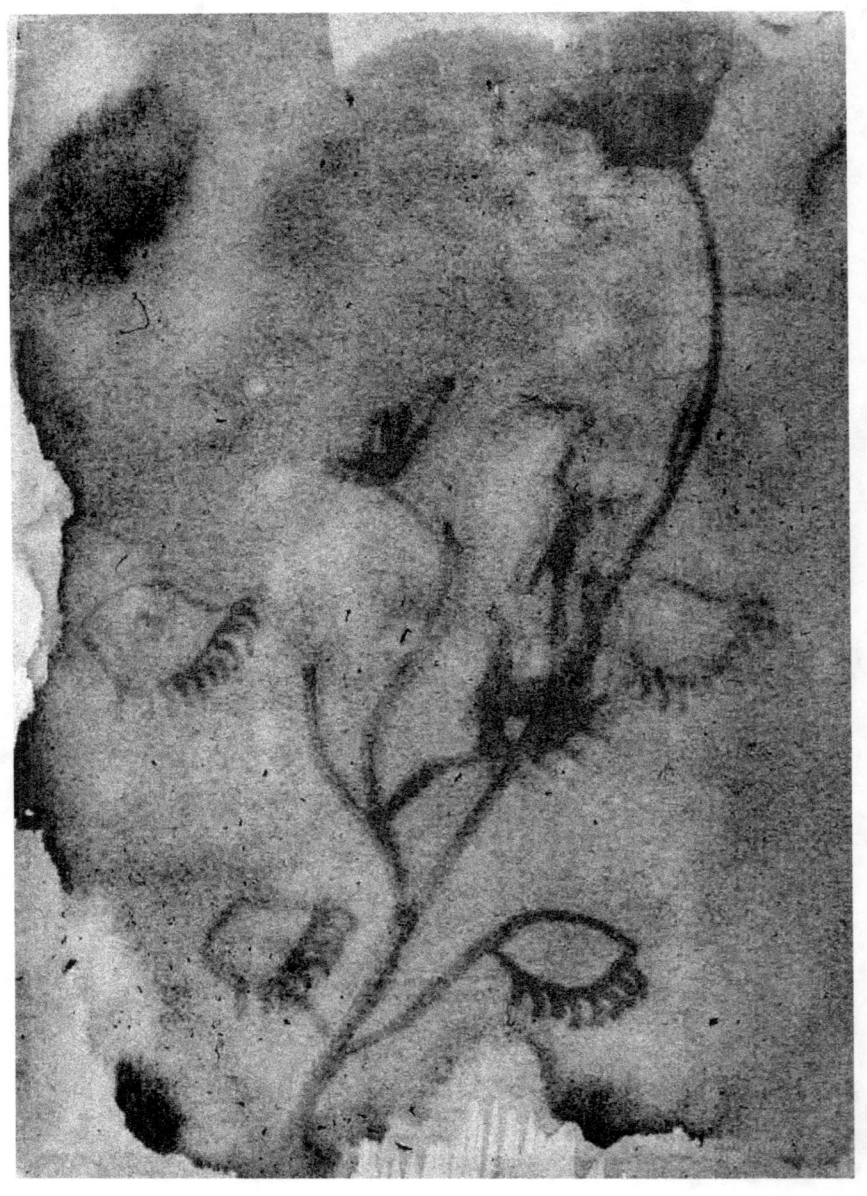

Black Licorice

Everyone spoke badly of you,
But I saw beneath it all.
I tasted you,
and nobody could believe
how highly I spoke of you.
It's clear, I'm the only woman who can handle you.
I can visit your darkness,
because I have my own
stash of black licorice.
Come along, come along,
we are thin and we are long,
we are tall and we are short,
we are fit and we are split.
We are all the types of hit and miss,
of black licorice.
Nobody wants even a little bit,
but we have each other
to taste and live with.
Fuck red licorice.

No Escape

What did you want?
when you invaded my mind
through just a paragraph
that lit my eyes
and woke up hope.
What were you thinking?
What made you think of me?
Asking spontaneously
to be at your feet
I was led to a game of pin the tail,
eyes blinded
and my heart robbed.
Soon before,
I became raw,
falling into the black hole of night.
Why did you push me into a hole of no escape?
That's exactly where you wanted me.
You didn't want me to leave.
You wanted me to soak up all you dumped,
You wanted me to endure all you made corrupt,
You wanted me to be all you needed—
And that, I definitely wanted to be

But not anymore
You put me in a black hole.
And I will never forget all you left,
Untold.

Where did you go?

Mammon

You explored the jungles,
even though I offered you gold.
You searched for more figures,
to double the dollar signs your eyes hold.

Oizys And The Foxes

Running miles at night,
to find cover.
Never being confident enough
to expose,
I remain undercover.
If you threaten me,
I'll attack.
I'm sorry,
My anxiety never made it easy to come
back
Come back.

Ella, My Love

Everything I loved,
you needed improved.
I fell to my knees
and asked for a guide
knowing well all I loved was
flawless.
I wanted you.
Scream the lines at me.
Tell me the path that links A to B.
Make me into a canvas, stretch
me along your frame, show me how to hold
all of you
right
here.
Tell me and I will listen
Tell me and I will flow in any direction you choose
because I have you to lose.

<u>Poseidon Pt.</u>

Being with you
felt like sinking into deep waters.
You were the rocks,
in my pockets weighing me down.
I was
sinking.
NO,
drowning.
Now, silently laying on the ocean floor.
Claiming my life is better with only you in it
Ignoring the truth, that I could rise without you.

Wandering Horus

You talk with your eyes.
It's your way of showing
you aren't focused on me.

Ode to a goddess

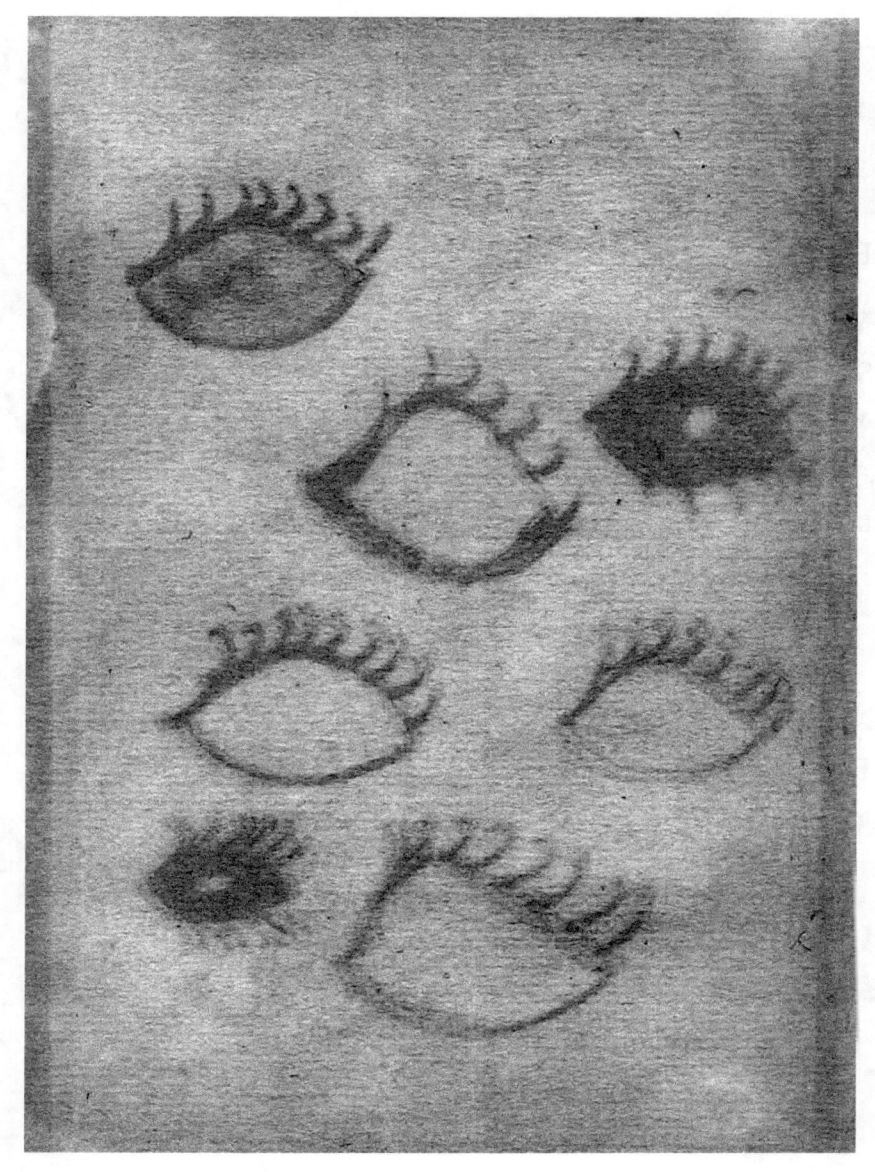

<u>Hypnos</u>

You left without saying a word.
Speechless— you left me without a sound.
You were muted.
And now I am trying to write about you
but how can I when all you projected was

Silence

My pain could speak
But even then,
you don't deserve it.

Sakura Boy

I know if you were to read this,
you'd feel so special.
You were always like that.
So confident,
always felt deserving, perky,
impeccable.
Always told me you deserved me
but I'll try my best to do the least
Because you were the worst,
and you did not blossom the way you promised.
Minus that Sakura from your name
because you were no cherry blossom.
You were the type to claim a blossom
when you were only in chase of the cherry,
without the bloom.

Clotho

Oh garment
how you form defeat when I apply you.
You empower my weakness
when I am hollow.
"-the power of fashion"

Snake Venom

I mastered your repetition,
rituals,
structure,
hissing.
I mastered you
And then I used that knowledgeable strength to move my joints
far,
away from you.
But even if you catch up
I'd be ready for you.
I'd catch you with my spade,
make it rain
the blood of yours,
 spilling in the rain.

Antaeus

Your temperature was past zero,
I had the last match
and you refused
All you needed, I had
but you did not want
to light yourself up
Confused, I lit
myself on fire
in hopes you'd see how bad I wanted you

Realisation

You joke too much,
you crave too much,
you craved so much,
you couldn't wait for me.
My innocence warmed you in places I never explored,
Places I didn't want to explore— yet
"Don't be mean to me!".
I may have given in,
if you only had waited.
You had access,
but you swiped
elsewhere.
You lost me,
the moment you shut that door and held her.
Not once, but twice.

christina antonia

A Song Dedication

Links to songs became a ritual of poetry,
then a ritual of melancholy.

*Gosh, these males are so smart
with their choices of dedicated song.*

I witness each redirection coming through, erasing the idea that it probably took you seconds to pick your way through. You found a sound, and a lyric that fits all —

that any girl could inherit. You all find songs that don't sit beneath you, in areas that your nails screech at — and voices that don't sing deep within you.

But I listened to those songs, with the intention of making them my home.

With the intention of playing them for so long
till they became my religion.

And then I asked you,

"Remember that song?"

And you turn around and said

"What?".

Hephaestus

So burnt,
so reused
I use the flame,
as a way to stay warm.
As a way to feel.
As a way to constantly see you.
Because of you,
I'm in hell.

Philia

Liquor taste
from your breath
Pillow talk
straight from those eyes
Support
 straight from the grip of my hands
"We have no title."
but cornered, overlapping bones, joints, lashes
And you claim we are just philia.

I Hoped To Save You

How bad I need you, blood.
How bad you needed the coke.
Why can't you see
you don't need it?
I needed you,
we needed you.
I'm sorry you believe I defeated you,
by screaming at you
and calling the police.
But we needed you,
to come home.
We needed the real you,
to come home
Without the coke.
because you're my blood.

Ode to a goddess

Boy Bel Air,

Touched his hair
to work in disguise, this love affair.
He doesn't even bother,
the noise in the air will call her,
the freak of the knight he rocked stands taller.
But she whipped and clashed,
removed his moustache,
with no push or gas to run to him in a flash.
Not one like you
can cop a feel
of a jewel with an eye of Horus
protected by providence.
She is not for you.
Her eyes see you.
You're a mouth with a sound,
no mind to be found.

Eros, From The Stories My Friends Tell

Nirvana has the power to
create black fireworks between the two.
Constant breathing, hot to the touch.
Eyes curve around you,
and you felt struck.
But then they dropped dead
And instantly they said
"That didn't last long,
I'm going to bed."

Sweet Addict

Sweet talk,
the words you used
like honey falling off a shiny spoon.
Onto my lips
into my mouth,
so frequent
that I developed
an obsession.
You empowered me but slowed me down,
tired me out with words engaged with zing.
But stung me, with nothing but sweet bullshit.
Leaving me without
any
energy
HELP ME.
I've blacked out.
I need to have you again.

Say No.

Candy— can you do?
Candy— can you do?

                                        But with who?

Candy— can you do me
what miss pixie did to who
on the enemies tube?

                                        No can do.

Damn.
Candy— cannot do
So I will fool
Around until I feel coo coo.
Candy— cannot do
What miss pixie did to who
On enemies favourite tube.

                              Then find you a pixie.
                              As that pixie is not me.

Libation

Poured directly into my mouth,
through my body.
Releasing the oxygen you held,
consuming my whole being.
You knew I'd consume you
in ways that weren't good for me—
because I wanted you.
And you chose to damage me.

What is it about you that resigned in me?
All this time?

The Husband of Aergia

You used beautiful music
as an excuse to not speak
your own beautiful words

Poseidon P2.

When his words become grey,
when he slowly begins to fade,
when it begins to push you deeper, under
listen to the voice waiting for you above water..

"FLOAT!"

Ludus

Falling for him
Is stripping naked in front of a crowd.
I show all of me,
but I don't want to
I want to stay within my four cream walls,
away from him.
I want to remain the persona I've made everybody believe.
Love is showing all of me,
and I don't want to.
I am made to be fierce
I know I am not.
But let it linger longer,
by making him believe in me
through a screen
with an act
that proceeds
to show my personality
that he cannot seem
to unleash.
When he finally sees me
I'll make him see I'm a mysterious woman.

Dicky

Hickory, Dickory, Dock
flaming shock he's got some jocks
what a shame he forgot his socks
now he's afraid to connect the Dots
or run outside to check the locks
Hickory, Dickory, Dock
this maniac has no Dosh,
he claims he knows whats under your cloth
but cannot stand on his feet with no socks
Hickory, Dickory, Dock
time goes by he's still in his jocks
boy oh boy, still no socks
my gosh he has no flipping rocks
to weigh him down or give him locks
to the treasures that remain in his jocks
He never even respected his own Damn Dicky,
Fuck out of here, boy in the jocks, so sticky

Isfet

Numb
But as firm as ever
Wounded
But as open as ever
Muted
But as colourful as ever
*Overcoming trauma

Mephitis

I am now careful
with scents
I need a shower
To get his smell
off
of
me.
Fuck
off.
F u c k
O f f.
Get
off
of
me.

Mania

Crazy

I know I'm crazy

I should unplug the plug in my waters

Raising, my waters raising—

To the thought of reaching out for more

Baby, I said baby, why won't you love me?

Leave me alone.

Crazy, you are crazy—

Fighting fish, threatening to reach for more

Cold and vulnerable—

on the floor, on my own.

I am crazy, I am crazy—

I did this all on my own.

Perses

You're a professional
bacteria
covering me
in all forms of horror—
bite and screech your way
right through me.
and I was dedicated to the process.
But I lost in the end—
because that's what people like you do, to innocent people like me.
You contaminate.

<u>Clapping</u>

Holding, resisting, tragedy.
What does it mean to fight the pink clarity?
With love comes stance, with heart comes dance.
What is it that you want from me?
Moisture, clapping, fists, dancing.
Did I perform a twirl in your cup of tea?
Holding resisting, tragedy.
Have you decided what you want from me?
Clap, one, two, three.
This is when you're meant to hold me.
Clap, three, two, one.
Fuck it, I'll never be your someone.

The Wasps Want The Honey

My Mother said, to chase what it is that calls—
but all that calls is melancholy and boys who half dress their physique.
Everyone tries to cut my locks, find their way past my socks. I say no,
I am a frigit bird, who knows nothing —how to do nothing— for this dude, who wants nothing
but to find their fingers into my honey. So Mother, do I listen to what calls? Please be clearer.
Because all these calls are not safe for my other her. The bees are buzzing —
and soon one will fight with her.

Ode to a goddess

christina antonia

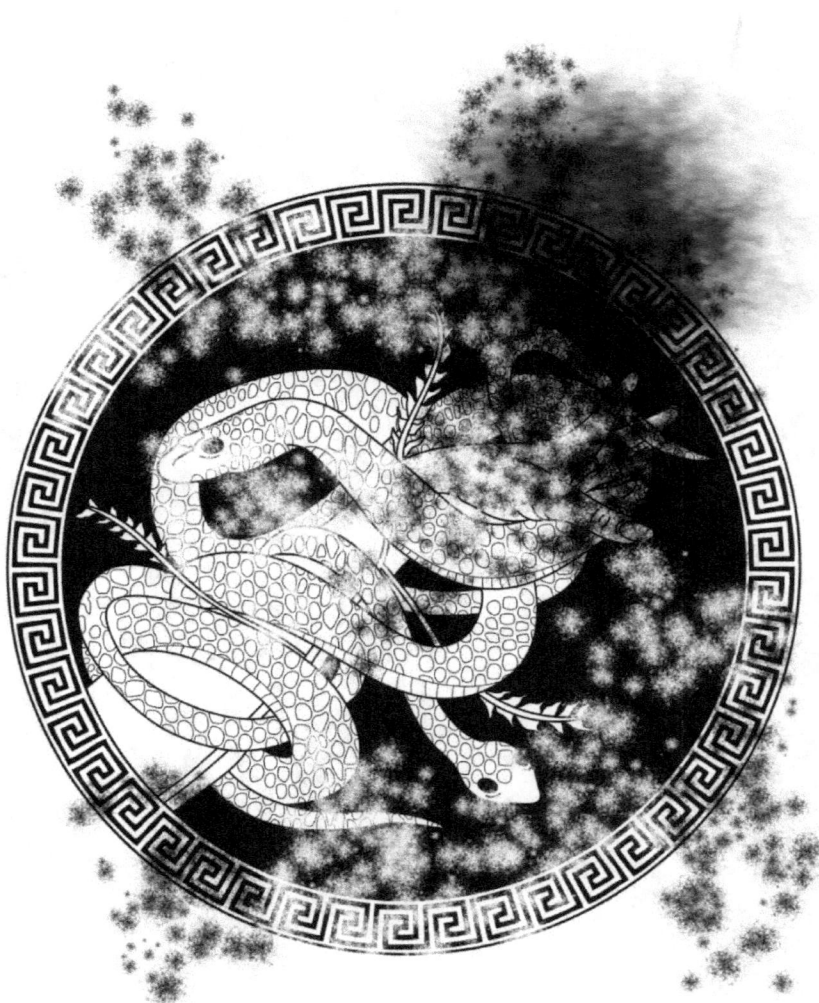

II. THE ANTISTROPHE
To turn black

Your **goddess** touch that you endured,
damaged
along the way.

Soft Fragments and traits,
Gentle badges that you'd wear,
Transformed to symbolise the enemy.

You're pitch black.

Not because of who you are,
but because of who the *world* can be.

The Year Dodeka

Weak,
diluted,
separating—
within the pressure.
Words go unheard,
and the pressure continues.
The strength—
like a grip
no, a GRAB
NO,
A
STRANGLE
around my throat.
They ask me to fall,
In—between the lines—
but that's *suicide*.
But the announcement of danger zones
and failed parachutes
cremates the remains of me.
And I fall,
because I gave in.
But even then, I didn't bother to be within the lines—
I had lost every fragment of myself
on the way down.

Cognition

I found you quietly
in my room.
You were within
black material and a tune.
You were formed by staring into the mirror,
wording words
and looking into my own eyes-

        moving,
            swaying,
                dancing.

You were found at 4am
in the bathroom
while I was thinking about the same old who.
You were formed when I became a character,
sealed with material on my skin,
a tune in my ear
and a who on my mind.
I became a walking cognition,
unlocking concepts and processes in my mind-
on my own terms
A walking source of power,
within my 4 cream walls.
Sealed in my world when the music is plugged in,
but brought back to reality when the earplugs come out.

christina antonia

Not a Simple Roar

But fuck it this year.
I want it all, I want it all to myself.
I won't keep it simple.
I am all in.
I don't want anyone to come in.
I'm forgetting I need to remember me,
but fuck it.
I don't care.
Nobody will ever be ready for me.
I have so much gas inside of me.
I keep pushing that latch even though I've hit full tank.
I don't care.
I will push it, until I explode.

until my heart stops,

until everyone floats away,

until I float away,

until my mind goes crazy enough

that I vomit

every single

thought and

creative idea

and bit of me

that I have left

because truth is,

theres nothing left.
But I push my chest,
an airless, lifeless chest,
Like a hopeful mother,
with their lifeless child,
in hope
they'd wake up soon.
Let me keep it simple,
So I don't have to face you.
I am not ready for anything—
But I will make you think I am.
I am gone—
But I won't let you see that.
I am finished.
But I won't let you see that.
I am completely numb—
but there's an endless world to feel
numb.

Let me keep it simple one last time,
I am not simple.

Green

I miss when green only meant
playing outside on the grass.
I miss the youth of not knowing
what comes after that.
I miss the freedom of not being
defined by how much of it you had.
I miss when green only meant
the leaves of a grapes branch.

Rise The Wolves

Distracted
by all the heads turning.
The ideas people make of the sounds they hear at night
"Is that howling?"
The way curves give the wolves something to run over, and combine as one,
to feed off of.
I ran across fields in belief of the purity of the lands
to be told that I am worthy
to bash,
turn,
scream and demand.
The pack was not of any good.
They claimed to know who I am,
but how could they when they had teeth
aimed to bite.
And I had teeth, made to soften the food
I brought for them to ignite.

Under The Influence

Just because I'm present, doesn't mean my mind is here.

Fire burning, I sip the idea of sin. The night was mellow, but I was not done. My mind as unclear as a window covered in rain. DROPS, my body drops beside the flaming fire that all these people surround. You sit there, girl. Girl, oh girl, I see with my stuttering eyes that you're about to have something to say. Gosh not you, I cannot stand the sight of you.

"Are you alright?"

Oh please, she's started. And you care because?

"Yeah I'm good, I'm just listening to this song and crying about a who."

Concealed

Broken glass,
distributed and pieced together
in the way you'd like.
I've taken back all my pieces and
shoved them together.
Drinking out of my own cup,
claiming to be the strongest,
the nastiest,
and most unique
Avoiding the knowledge that I'll break soon,
With all the cracks that remain.
I will stain the only white surface
that remains.
And then you will see, I am not all I claim to be.
With the drink spilling through
whilst I continue to conceal my boo boo's.

Fuckery

Fucking with my head
until I'm mislead.
Fuck the fucking fucker that fucked off
all that I had left.
I fucking blame the people around me,
for the fuckery that fucks with my head.
But everyone around me tells me,
I am the one fucking with my head.
Yeah.
YOU.
YOU
are the one that fucks with yourself.
YOU
are the fucker to blame.
YOU
were all you had left.
YOU
are the fuckery that mislead
YOURSELF.

christina antonia

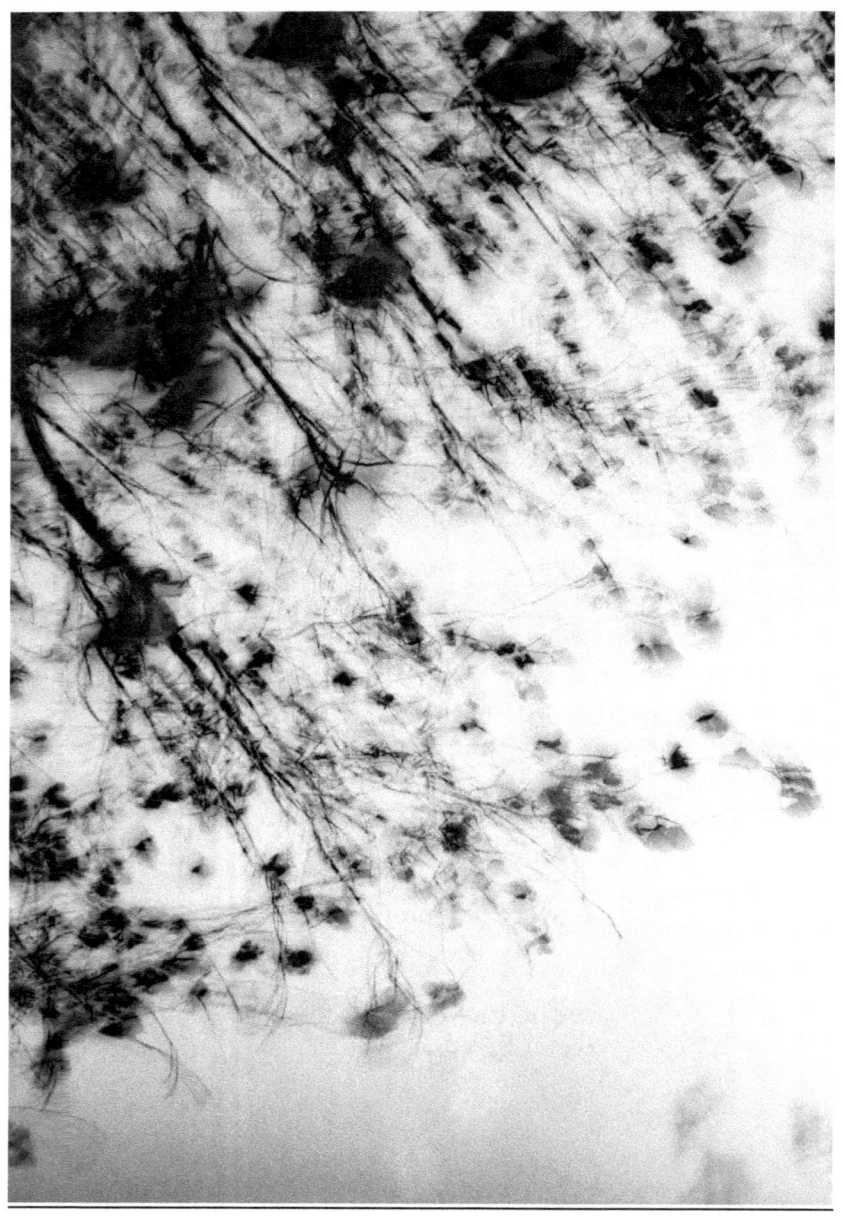

Ptah in Ruins

Pain designed
formulated,
pampered
and charming.
Oh, how you drive me to be a walking piece of art.
Designed to destruct,
and create.
Designed to stop everybody,
for them to take a look.
Yeah,
maybe a step closer—
but that little step closer
makes the alarms go
OFF.
And
    I
       will
           liquidate
               and
                   self
                       destruct.

Escape

Running through me like the thought of
wanting the world in my hands.
Enduring all that I need and want
to reach a high point of
happiness and demand.
The difference is
I wake up,
mascara creating a black filter—
Trying to escape
back into the dream state I was in
before the pressure of my surroundings became
more than real.
Escaping reality is no longer magical.
It is a desperate call for help,
away from what I don't want to be a part of

Mur Mur

I hear voices in silent places,
At 5am, in corners of the room I have been facing.
Carnivals in my mind, with the fame I have been chasing
No step on the wood, of the plank that waits for me
on a daily basis.
I am living as a performer, in the walls of my bedroom,
pretending to be an elite with a Midas touch.
I am worth the gold,
when I have not even left my house.
I am worth the gold,
even with the belief that
being in my own mind is enough to have
the touch that is worth more than a self-absorbed brat.

Dolus

Nobody can know my strengths but me,
because it's all I have left.
Sharing this last part of me,
would mean I have nothing left for me.
And here it is.

<u>Winter</u>

The warmth has fallen,
Autumn to be.
I have woken up
from a cold case mystery.
I hear voices mourning me,
children run from me,
under the covers—
warm and feisty.
They beat at my beetroots,
they who don't fond me so
I say goodbye
to those mockeries.
I'll be fine—
bleeding till spring shows.
Only some know the divine.

christina antonia

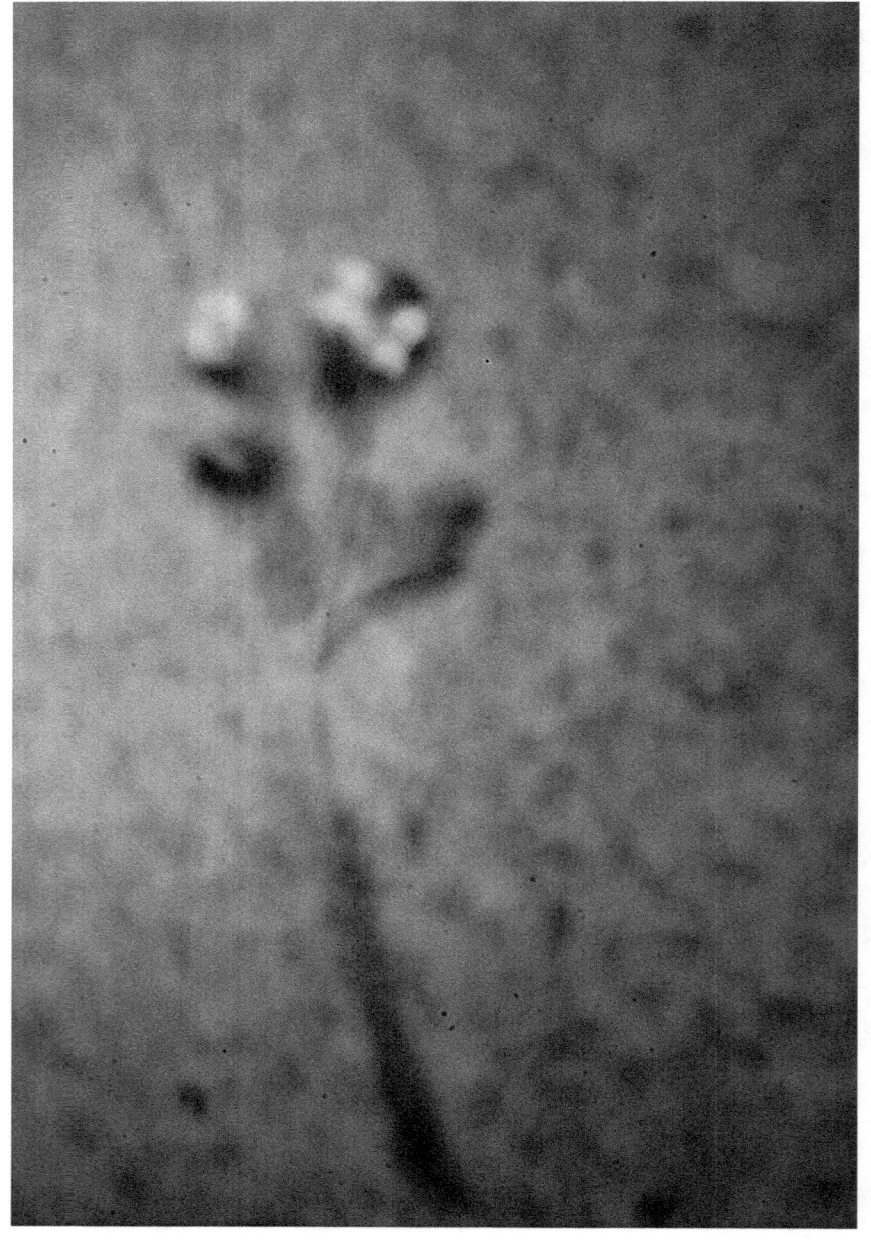

Not on Drugs, I Would Never

Just losing my mind to a whom
losing hydration from my face to a who
and just sick and tired, of that who.

> *Mum, I'm not on drugs.*
> *It's just someone.*
> *Someone who sucks all the life out of me,*
> *Leaving me soulless, rude and hefty.*

The Only Time Recycling Isn't Okay

Sick
of feeling refurbished
every few days.
of being told
how happy they were to have picked and chosen me.
Instead given away,
by one minor update
in appearance.

Melodrama

Charisma
in their speaking voices,
to elevate the shepherd within them.
Pushing the sheep, shoulder to shoulder
until all sides the sheep considered, are zero.
And a part of the lifeless herd, you make them.
One way lead by the shepherd.
Through the terror and the horror, drama,
of what you want.
The black sheep, is incapable
because of the poisonous lure of dependency.
No matter if it kills them,
you guide them,
with your eye of providence
until
they
descend
under.

Back and forth,
like a joke.
You push and shove,
and scream
"FUCK".
And dream
and lose
and gain
and fuck up.
And say no
and say yes
but say
"BUT."
You have lost them,
the moment you closed the gates,
and blinded their direction
and held them.
"No, they didn't hold me".
There was no modesty blanket.
You strangled them,
and pestered them,
until they were struggling from mayhem.
And they became lifeless,
was it worth it?

christina antonia

Religion in a Dream

The car span
with my mother and I in it
I was sure we were going to crash
but it all went silent.
I began to spin
down a tunnel,
and these faces I feared
wanted to be faced.
God,
please don't be mad
that I've claimed to be amongst another.
For I'm sure you are not
a being of one,
but a being of everyone.
If I am right, God please don't punish me—
for the decision I've made to convert.
Someone had to lay down and be
vulnerable when nobody else would be.

Medusa

They scream,
"Hey MEDUSA!
I see you!
With your ugly hair!
Hey Medusa, Medusa!
Going somewhere?
Medusa, Medusa,
Going to chop your hair?
Medusa, Medusa,
Ugly hair!"

                I say
"Don't fuck with Medusa, Medusa,
Come closer.
Medusa , Medusa,
What did she do wrong?
Medusa, Medusa,
Leave her alone!
Medusa, Medusa,
Turn you to stone!
I mean, I told you not
To fuck with Medusa
But now that you have,
You probably wished you didn't.".
Time to take another to the closet,
Rock hard, rock hearted
Along with all the others.

Ode to a goddess

Poltergeist P1.

You've made wars, poltergeist
in attempt to distinguish your pain—
in a continuum of acts— to ruin all that I've flourished.
But I warn you
Of my freakish nature.
The only act that can adhere to my skin
is my own.
Every move made by you—
won't attach.
Stones thrown,
with no show of your appearance—
all to show people the damage you've made.
Nobody can see you.
There is nothing to gain.
I repeat,
I warn you of my freakish nature.
I warn you of my freakish nature.
I warn you of my freakish nature.

Ode to a goddess

I am the only source who can hurt me.
You can bother but you cannot gain
a
single
thing
from
this

apart from ruining your own chances at peace.

The Death Blame

You can blame the sharps tools
that were used to damage a livelihood
on yourself.
Yourself being the one who was always within four walls,
hallucinating hopelessly,
away from monstrous beings.
How could it have been your fault
when all you encountered was a dream?

Death Bees

There comes a time when, the bees keep on humming—
Singing till they're pouring all their sweetness away.
I felt it that night.
When the world around me grew by thread,
then by trunk,
then eventually with people's hands.
You grow this trust in others, so much that it seems
Impossible—
that the idea of sweetness in the world could fade soon.
Well it did.
And I am still shocked, by the memory of holes
in the ground
dedicated to man,
who were never meant to leave the world yet.
I could imagine the bees and bugs that swarmed your head,
when you decided to bury a man half alive,
deep beneath the thread.
What were you thinking when you killed your mate,
boofhead?

Death Noises

Some music
became sounds of pain.
The crackling in instrumentals,
The low wows,
the deep humming voices—
became violent.
Sounds and music of aesthetic—
became reasons to hear murder,
became reasons to fear songs I loved.
Vibrations became ticks,
of imagining what you went through.
Tied up and driven to a mountain,
Found skeletonised and unrecognisable.
A familiar face became a
delusional enemy
to you,
And your loved ones.
Noises
became a tick
a trigger to the idealism of what you
went
through.
Fuck that coward, we won't forget you.
———

R.I.P Cayleb

My Best Friend Never Listened to Me

Worshiped and honoured,
a fuck wit, a coward
that taught her that her legs were banter.
There it is, a scream.
There it is, her seams—
dangling by the bed it seems.
There she goes,
there he goes,
fortressing the curves of the banjo.
Ring a ding, ring a ding,
calling for another fling.
Ring a ding ring a ding,
he loves then he flees.
"Don't say "I told you so".".

Eat It

I say to myself,
eat it all up,
to the point of nothingness-

but don't show it.

Show that it's making you grow

in success-

although it's only making you slower.

Eat it up,
your assumptions of others perceiving you as less
when all they do is say nothing to keep away-
because of your cold waters.

Eat it up,
your idealism of what is happening around you.

And you're stuck with a slow mentality and physical physique.

You took the cake and ate it -
so much that nobody is around
to have their share.

You forgot about everybody.

and you thought you didn't forget about yourself,

but you did.

The moment you destructed your strengths
of love and care.

Ode to a goddess

You believed in being a fool to the world,
when it was a fool to you,
as if this would strengthen you.
But it did not.
You were scared you'd be left with nothing
And you were.
And you were selfish.
But you didn't know any better.
I blame you,
and I don't blame you.
This was your lowest point Christina.
I know death ruined you.
But you ruined those who tried to fix you
You lost your goddess senses that particular year—
and you can't take it back now.
You can only hope to build yourself back to the light you were supposed to be and always were.
You became the darkness that visited you.
Never let yourself go back there.
And never let the world's darkness remove your light,
ever
ever
again.

christina antonia

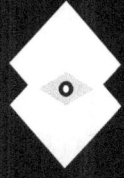

III. THE EPODE
Said after

Softly rising again —
the gentle **goddess** in you.
You are escaping round two.

This is what it means to
remember —
the soft lady you were made to be.

Traits of kind, mothering and ode.
Stay within this zone,

never leave.

Poltergeist P2

Having a moment within your own silences—
speaking to yourself,
and realising your demons.
Seeing them in poltergeist forms,
and accepting them as they are.
They are so angry and so afraid,
but you set them to ease.
I began to close my eyes.
I wrapped them in cream silk,
and squeezed my favourite perfume upon them.
I reminded them that they are the darkest parts
of my spice blend.
I reminded them that they will always be there.
Yeah, you.
You will be there to haunt me sometimes, and I will allow you
with open arms to enter my house.
I won't force a door closed on you anymore,
because I accept you with every inch of me.
My heart won't weigh you down anymore.
I just want to comfort you and remind you that there is kindness still left.
I won't hope for you to change, because you have been molded
through trauma.
But I love you.
And I will take care of you.
Because things are different now.
I will love you more than I have ever loved before.

Ode to a goddess

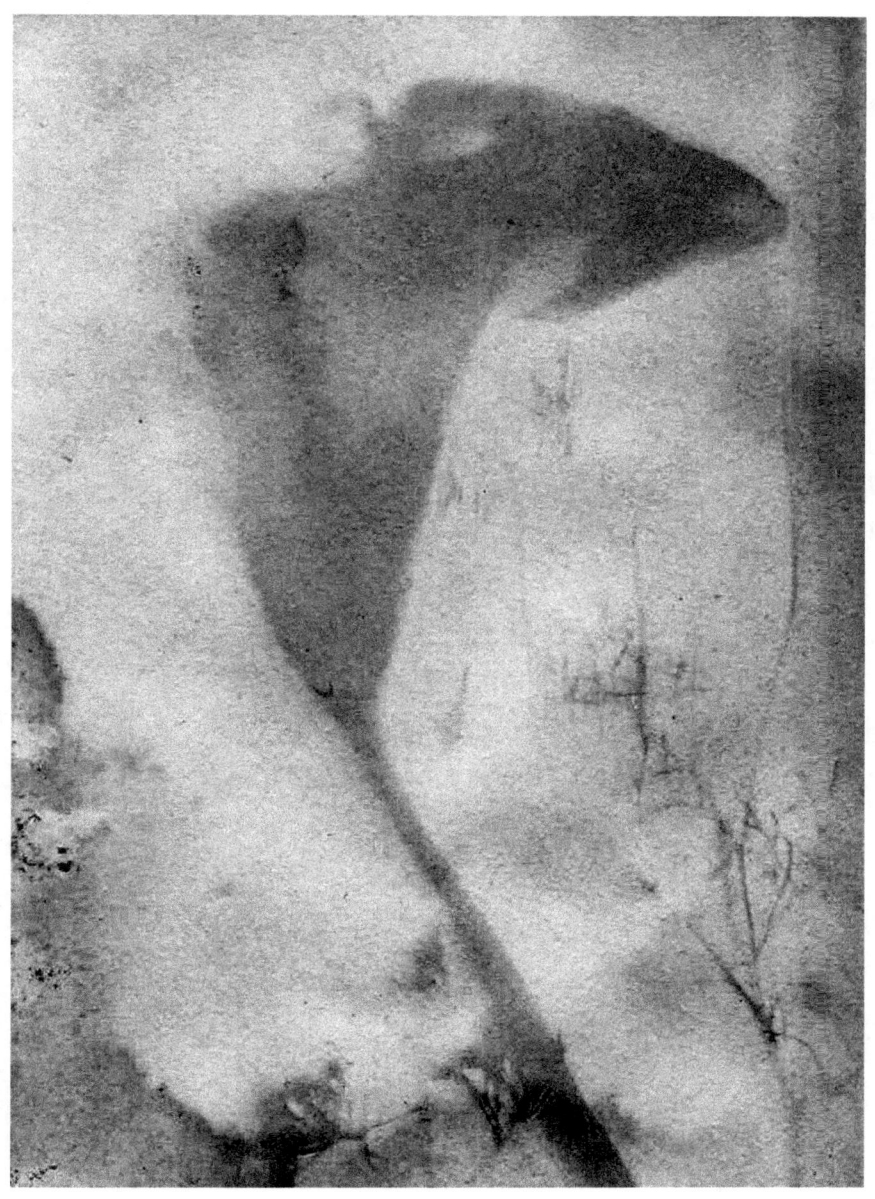

Shield of Athena

I write in pain,
but pain has been terminated.
I mean,
my view of pain has been terminated—
and replaced with the knowledge that
every shred of blood,
every liquid that escapes my two eyes
appeal to the shield that I wear—
and assist my walk in life.
Through my ancient history,
through my recent history,
and pain and poltergeists that follow me—
comes a walking matriarch,
and her Shield of Athena.
Through everything that may attempt to bite,
I will strike
with kindness.

Aphrodite

Cherry cheeks
how I missed you.
Life in my skin.
The glow, the sparkle
of the knowing.
Yes, you know that woman.
She is Alive, plumped
and ready to spread butter—
through people's hard ends
and dry spots.
You are soft,
you are filled with white petals
that fall behind you,
when you walk into a room.
I missed you.
I rose to the surface
when you remembered
that your gentle ways
is the real you, Christina.

christina antonia

Mother Gaea And Her Jasmine

Picked me up in my sleep,
in my most unknown stages.
Filled me with your gentle rain
drops, drop, drops,
that helped me bloom.
You spoke gentle whispers in my ears
of guidance from the man above
who loves us all.

                        "Forever and ever, Amen.",
                              Together, we say.

Dressed me in white silver
to keep me safe from the thieves.
But with gold running through my veins—
only I can enter the stems, it seems.
Jasmine filled up your gardens,
as a youth.
You decided to bring your own Jasmine to earth.
Releasing sweet nectar,
before father made you seem like a fool.

                " You gave me the strength to leave him!",
                                    Mother said.

The scent of Jasmine was your alibi—
When father took all, and left not even a cent.
So you made sure that scent remained for good.

       " You wont be alone, I promise!",
             I reply.

Jasmine is my name
 And so is the flora
you have given me
for the rest of my days.
Jasmine was almost my name.

Deceive

Do you know what's best for me?
Do you have the key that will be used to enter inside?
Do you think your unique path is a way to mine?
Do you believe we don't have time?
Do you see what it is you're doing to me?
I don't think you do.
You deceive me
and you deceive every
body.
You are unaware of the pillars that have resigned in you-
and you have stood with them like a fool.
Green, green, green
they say to me.
Steer up side
and down side
do a 360.
Forget what you first began with
and what's to be—
a shiny life,
and house with a palm tree.
Lock yourself up
because this is the means to be

a proud mama's son's, grand trophy.
Inhale and exhale, your pride to be
is this how you pictured your life to be?
Run as fast as you can and remember to be
open minded and open hearted
remain free
use your voices to scream and show everybody
you will not be congested,
and small,
and nothing.
You will be heated, loud and defined.
So bold and so proud and so magically free
Find yourself patience to find the right thing
or person or trace of what you will be.
The choices you make will never be doubted,
when you are making gestures that suit your insides.
Healing and building to the point of no fear,
you are what you've been missing since you stopped here.

In Your Eyes

I form a recognition
between you and I.

Our eyes sink deeper through the stare
and the ride through you intertwines—
our finest
lines.

christina antonia

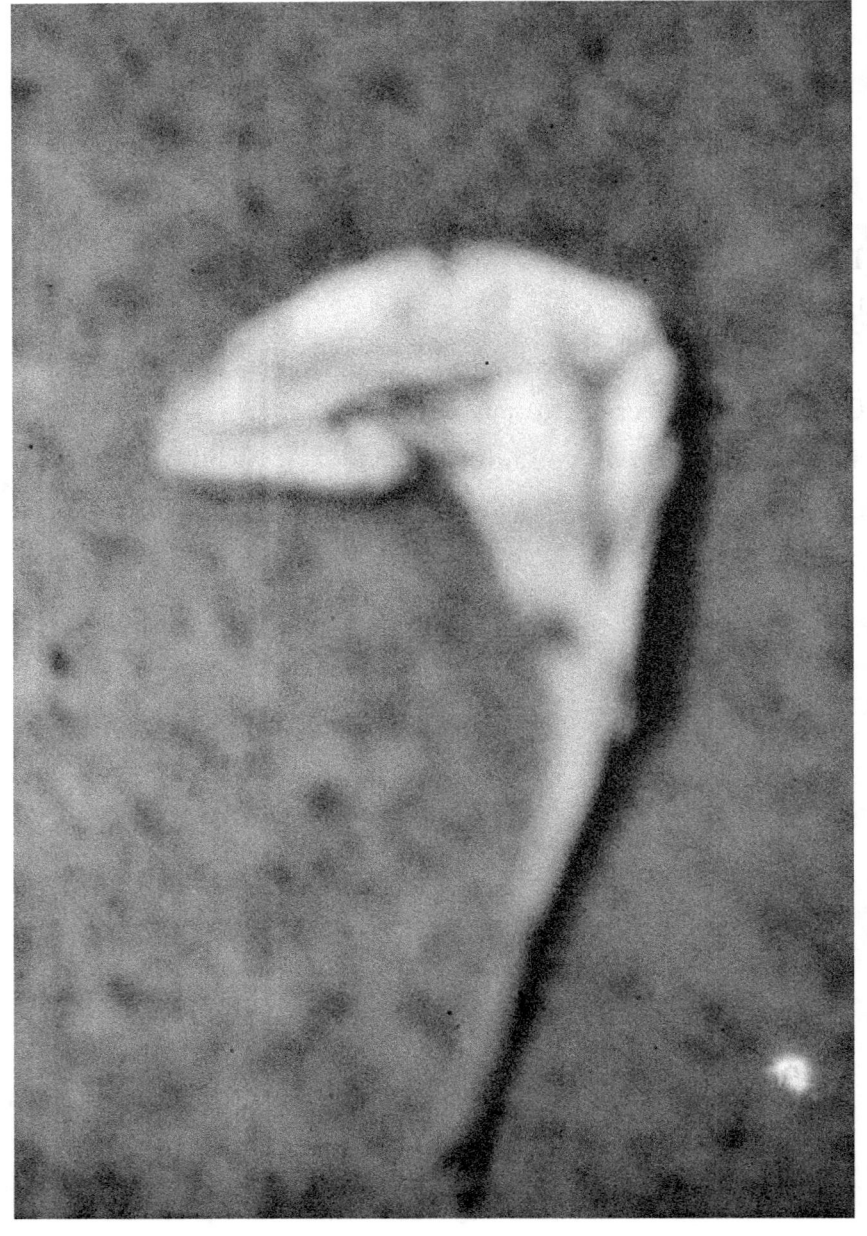

I appreciate people when they go

Whether it comes with age,
whether it comes with fear,
whether it comes with distance.
We lose touch,
so quickly, so gently, without purpose.
So accidentally, that when you realise,
you will not be ready.
Many brought me to incredible awe,
but this was only accessed when
we all had a half meeting point.
Now our points are finished
and the meeting is no longer.
And I miss you.
And I miss many.
And I thank every person who has stayed with me,
in my mind.

A Black Rose

Re-defined
from its concept of dark—
to it's idea of strength.
A black rose,
combination of all the colours
and more.
Overlapped,
with experience
shades, bright pops and tones
A modern global norm,
we pin them proudly.
For now, it is experience,
that defines us.
Not the gentle,
the pretty
or the demi.

Ode to a goddess

Grand Athena

Grand success
is not within the stacks of green value.
It is within your human self,
your soul and time with others,
as it is all you take to your grave.

Semo Sancus

Your glasses are painted black,
And you can no longer see,
from the buildup of fear and aggravation.

And damn, you really need those glasses to see
What effects how I see,
also effects how you see.
You choose to stand still in the darkness
and wait until
I have the energy to stand
beside you,
and clean them for you.
You keep on waiting—
happily, remain,
happily, keep me.
No matter if that means waiting in the pitch black.

Ode to a goddess

Prick

A rose
with a sign
you believe says "take one".
But one with common sense will know,
you are stripping her of her beauty—
and growth
by objectifying her.

Daisy Field

A foundation of flora
made to display
A colony of strength.
If seen, one, on its own—
perceived
small,
fragile,
less of its value.
If seen together—
perceived differently.
Perceived strongly,
by the paparazzi.
All hands on deck,
all together now—
create a perfect picture
to be a team now.
But overtime
with persistence,
comes the educational value.
So, when left alone
the world will see you for your collaboration
and then your independent value.
—— Women, do not give up.

Ode to a goddess

Tomb

How you have formed around me,
and have continued to shape around the youth.
The younglings
with developing minds-
are screaming to come out from inside.
Remain in history where you belong,
and allow them stretch
and to take up space.
They will find room beyond the classic tomb.

You Do Not.

You do not have to stay sane
You do not have to find ways to remain like the fame portrayed.
You only have to be one.
Who stands present with you now?
Tell me about your mind, and the thoughts that you visit.
How you have fallen in the shower, accidentally balancing too much on a one-foot-shave trip.
What is it that you love and think about in the shower when there is no sound to entertain your mind?
Where are the places you visit when the world is not so kind?
Whatever it may be, know that I am soft enough to listen and that you are allowed to drip your water on my towel after your lonely shower—
Please listen.
A woman once told me,
being a wild goose is the case to
finding peace within your insane.
No honk is ever the same.
So be loud,
little goose.

The God With an Achilles Heel

Vulnerability is not weakness,
in the right mind,
with the right knowledge,
with the right people.

<u>Vanilla</u>

In all her mighty,
She is predicable.
She's been around long before your Mother had you.
She is part of the news,
She is part of no trend,
She never has to renew, like what you said.
She is the same, over and and over again.
She is to blame? No, no-one can agree with that.
She is the one that everyone knew long before you.
She is preferred over your extravaganza.
She is simple, precise, everyone likes that.
She is boring? No, no-one can agree with that.
She is memorable, ain't
nobody
going
to
match
with that.

"So can I have Vanilla, please?"

White Linen

Protect me
Shield my fresh skin.
Warm me
When I lose consciousness and rest.
Hide me,
Respect that I'm underneath
and I'll lay here
at peace.
— Safe Love

How to Make Passionfruit

Passionate.

Passion in it.

Pass on with it

Pass it on with you in it.

Cherry Wine

Consuming you,
drop by drop.
Gently moving across my back,
doing rounds around my temples
to slowly land in places that leave stains of
purple grape and sweetener.
We squeeze and smell, until it has consumed our silent senses.
My cherries begin to drop
all over the surfaces—
bursting and leaving stains
We are art.

The Ideal Parachute

With arms crossed over,
in a circle full of people—
you grab hands,
anybody's hands,
and hold tight.
The sea is about to worsen,
the sea begins to rock.
We all hold on,
without a second thought of judgement
of who's hands we hold.
We hold through the worsening weathers
and happily stand strong when the sun comes out.
This is commitment.
this is a team,
And we don't judge here.
We keep you safe,
when you fall.
There is no two faced.

Ode to a goddess

Yiya Christina

Oh Tina,
how sweet, you made tea for me.
Oh Tina,
how sweet, you got chamomile for me?
Oh Tina,
It seems, I have tingles all over me.
Oh Tina,
It seems, I am fading, soon to be beneath.

>My Yiya, my Yiya
>Of course, there will be tea.
>My Yiya, oh Yiya,
>chamomile with 4 sugars in your tea.
>My Yiya, poor Yiya,
>don't speak so poorly.
>My Yiya, my Yiya,
>listen to me carefully.
>"Agape Mou!", you call me
>But Agape Mou, it is now for me to say to you.
>Allow me inside, to navigate your mind.
>Allow me to be the one to make you decide
>whats best for you.
>My Yiya.

Drastic Motions

Danger zone
it seems.
The roles and
the love
and the kindness.
After first handedly experiencing
Tragedy—
How can you be soft again?
Please,
re-evaluate,
and re-define
the already existing
protocols and lines.
Create and birth
your own vines
and swing from them.
Swing high,
and higher.
Create new motions
and wave lengths—
for those who are young
and in need of your influence.
You are the new drastic motion.

Not Just

A lilac pulsing vein,
not just the nerve that tells you it'll rain,
not just a hug that feels the same
as everyone else.
Not just a symbol of rose,
nor a crimson, dark moon show,
not just a boy that guides you home
and then leaves you.
He is a fruitful, fluttering zing.
Yeah, the one that makes you sing
when you finally win
uno.
He is an apple that grows,
and isn't afraid to roll,
and roll and roll
far from the tree.
Girl, when it is finally your turn
and you speak murmur and yawn,
he better like you when you yearn
and think freely.

Ode to a goddess

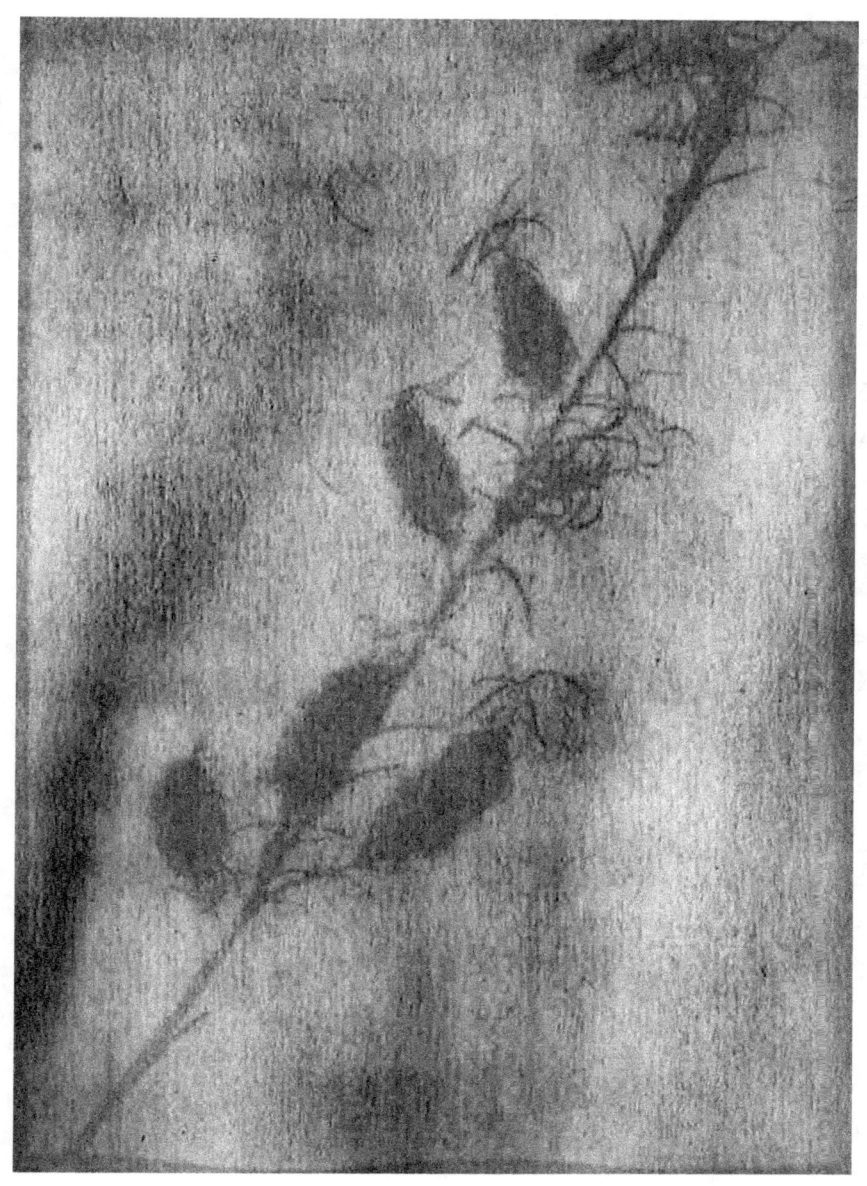

Teething

Pushing and trying,
soothing and biting,
keep trying and trying.
You feel it coming -
the pressure and numbing,
the timeless crying,
inflaming your mouth.
You can't speak
you can't be,
who you want to be,
when the oppression peaks.
The skeleton that grows from you
may be crooked or straight,
either way,
Once the growth is finished—
you will have amour to bite bait.
But also, to soften the debate.
Mishaps will turn into skeletons,
another reason to show those pearly teeth.
So child, please, be safe in between
the sheets and the kitchen and the in-between where we meet.
Stay within cotton and warm cups of tea.
Let the year change again until you become
teethed.

Villains Only Tighten Their Teeth

"Don't crunch your teeth!"
mother said.
"They begin to form crooked teeth."
"Don't scrunch your face!"
mother said.
"It begins to frame your signature head."
"Don't speak of the mean!"
mother said.
"It begins to consume the believes in your head."
"Don't allow it in!"
mother said.
"Allow your teeth to peek through your lips instead.".

Parfum

The Intro

Within an aroma
Came a sense of the past
A sense I could not rid
As the sense has locked in my mind
Through my veins and into my heart

The Body

I've changed my mind.
Perfumes are not boring gifts.
Well, a handful of you made it seem so, a little bit.
But if you pick with intentions,
And you pick with love,
And you gift that scent to someone,
That gift is not just a scent.
It is a memory that will never leave or be absent.
Once inhaled, I will either think of you
Or remember a time I wore it out
With you
Or Without you
Or in my happy place
Or in my sad space.

The Outro

Perfume is not a boring gift.
Perfumes are part of an underdog amour
Pick wisely, as it's all your memory will battle with
Forever.

Young Amour Misconception

Never mind your young exterior,
shine your light regardless of how small you feel.
If it is important,
make people aware.
If it is important,
breathe in,
breathe out.
and shout it out.

christina antonia

Sleepy Lavender

Flower scent,
Lilac beams,
Relax on my shoulder.
Lavender burns in the air at 2
AM, it's just for you.
Soft feet exterior.
I feel my blankets heating up
From the person that sleeps near.
Lavender make me sleep.

christina antonia

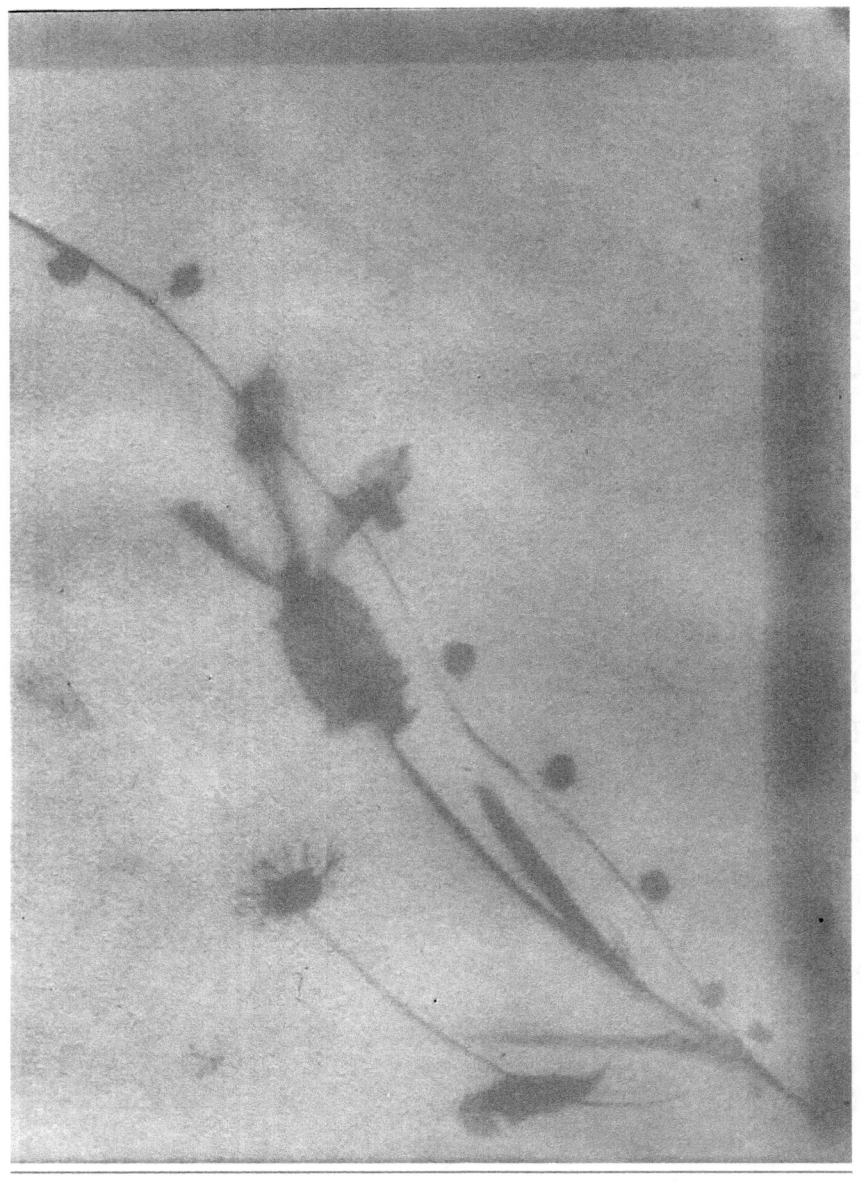

Ode to Esther

Flavoured Esther I taste.
Softness was never only felt,
but consumed.
I swallowed it at the peak of understanding
the words that came out of my father's mouth.
I was praised as the angel that came to save us.
Was I meant to undo the knots
already tied,
before I even knew the blue sky?
The screams of my only brother.
I was once dancing rings around my father.
But the then world span around me, over a multitude,
and then I sank and learned,
that circles can create knots.
And knots cut circulation—
of the smiles of the women most close to me.
The blood stopped circulating the bodies that raised me,
I created lengths between father
and me—
I had hopes to start the circulation
and cut the cycle.
Brother, I may not seem soft, Esther.
Like the girl who once danced rings around my father.
But I have gained the armour the women,
who raised us,
never had the courage to wear.

christina antonia

How to Be a Poet

Contaminate the floors. Crack in the wall. Earrings dangling, now they're on the floor. Spicy, pumpkin, cinnamon. Is that all? Gestures and twists that hint human kiss. Root for cascade living, but preferred a graffiti hometown. Cherry lip stain to speak graphically. Camera man can only take one pic. Hey, you, can I have a sip? Pompeii, Amaretto, Brandy. Heavy licking whipped cream.

Leak what is in, out into your cup.

Pour it on your surfaces. Spice it up.

Champagne

Lollies bubble up the hips,
finding its way into a kiss,
this is what it means to taste test this.
Parading down the street alone,
spinning and twirling to the thought of you alone,
I wear my demi wispies
and finally plump my cheeks.
Ready to see you,
the butterflies know this.
The bubbles of champagne gas me up,
till you're in sight.
I crave the wind that will hit me,
when you move your arms
towards me
and manage to freely
give me a hug.

Neptune's Vanilla Cone

Reoccurring wave lengths,
but in different shapes and sizes.
The same so we recognise you
but unpredictable.
Every year,
we come to see you–
because that's love.
And our love for you is very much the same
every year.
You love somebody, and suddenly all of their vanilla attitudes.
Something about it -
the aspects of the flavour,
you wouldn't mind tasting over and over.
The timelessness becomes irreplaceable.

Ode to a goddess

Dear Jillian Banks

I've thinking it over,
the way you came and changed
the world and made me sane.
You gave it all
when they made me *colder*—
when I wished I was in love
but all I did was face the pain.
You showed me *what it feels like*
to *drown* but stand up and face the *change.*
I hit *under the table,*
but you flowed your *warm water* underneath -
and I gave you a peek.
Mother Earth, you were destined to be
the one who would love and *haunt* me.
Screech at me in my sleep, when you knew it wasn't for me.
You were protecting me
when I seemed a *weak girl.*
The only *poltergeist* seemed
to want the right thing for me.
I fucked with myself

and you held me
told me to see
I had always been
A *goddess* and will always be.
You *stroked my ego*
when it needed to be
but stopped me in my peak.
Because this ego was not for me,
it will ruin me.
Took me to *Hawaii*
amongst all my *mazes*
and made me see
all this *contamination*—
was from a place that I didn't choose.
But from *the fall* that made me roar.
You gave me what I wanted,
when I didn't know it myself.
You continue to tell me

You're a goddess.

Ode to a goddess

Day of Rest

Here comes the sun,
and it feels different.
Silent mornings and vibrations,
soft and humid.
Love vibrates through soft morning voices
and gentle sounds of movement —
love almost advocates the description of Sunday
through history.
Sunday is the day we lay
We pray and we remind ourselves
Hey,
Whose words are to say
we cannot *rest* on this day?
We are getting lost in the fast movement
that begins when we step outside.
But don't be ignorant, when you notice
the silent air and motions when you first wake.
In our hearts we know,
today, Sunday,
is the end & the beginning
of Both a safe haven and a fresh start.
of a week.
Allow the sunlight to warm you,
and rest, please rest.
Tomorrow is the day you can wake, be fresh
And start again.

Ode to a goddess

For Your Thoughts

christina antonia

Ode to a goddess

christina antonia

Ode to a goddess

christina antonia

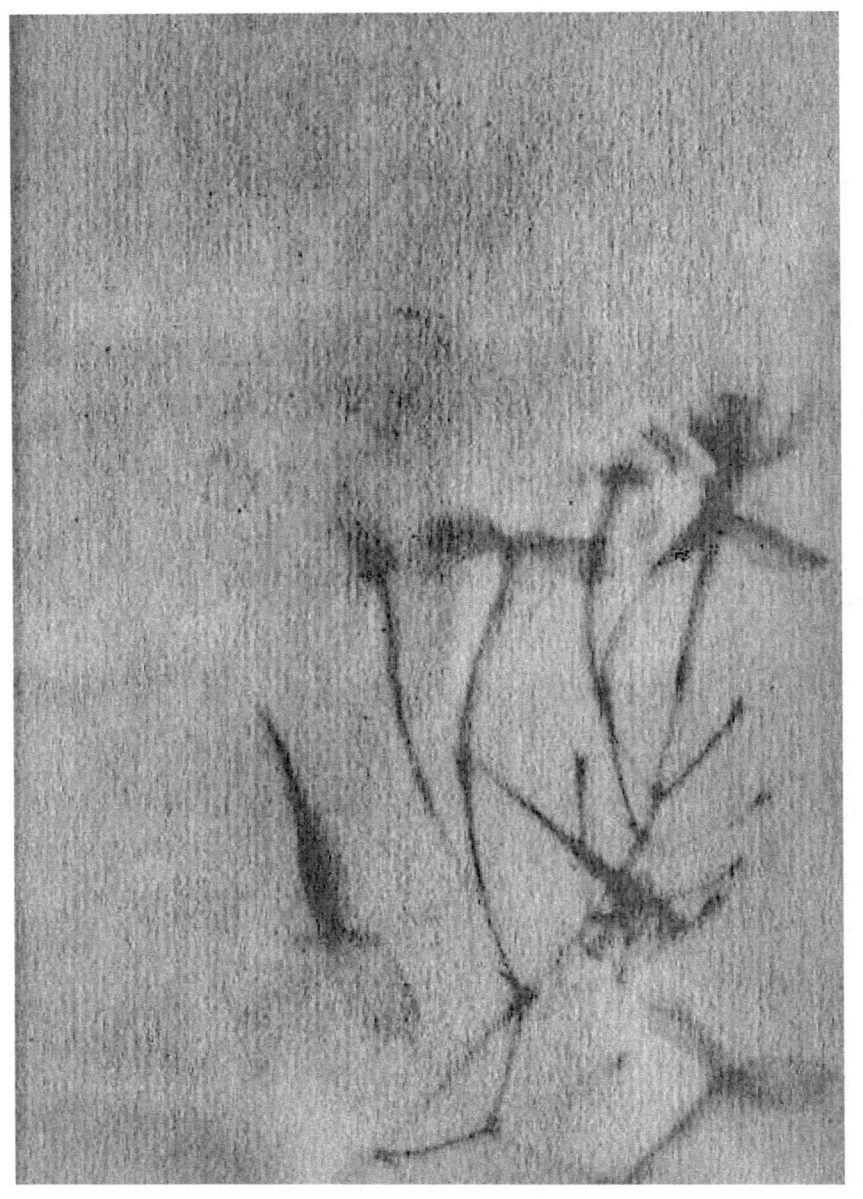

Ode to a goddess

Ode to a goddess

christina antonia

Welcome to The End of This Collection

Allow me to thank you for your patience and care while reading this book.

You've experienced all of it with me. I hope you're feeling okay!

Connect with me, show me the writings in this book that you connected with the most. I would love to know you related to one of them.

Find me, speak to me, have vulnerable chats with me - and tag any poems that you resonated with via Instagram @christinantonia.

I hope to hear from you soon.

Love,

christina antonia

One Last Thing

Do as many things as you like, even if it is out of what you usually do. Even if people question why you're doing it. Even if it doesn't make sense to the life you have built.
Truth is, you can do anything.
At any time.

About Imagery

Anthotypes: Several images made from natural flora juices, real sunlight. Painting thick paper with natural juices from coloured petals/ vegetables that have been mashed and squeezed of their juices. This juice is what you paint your paper — to act as paint. Applying your object or flora ontop, then placed in a frame in sunlight for several days. The surrounding juice around the object will fade from the sun and leave a print of the object.

Digital Pinhole: A process of creating a lens with a very fine hole and Aluminium foil. Using a DSLR camera, purchase a camera body cap that you can use to drill a hole into. On the inside, tape Aluminium foil over the hole. Poke a mini hole with a sewing needle. Screw the cap onto the body of your camera. This is now your digital pinhole lens. Blurry imagery can be captured.

Mirrorless Imagery: Simply taken on a Canon RP and a 50mm lens - on a black and white setting.

All imagery made by Christina Antonia

www.ingramcontent.com/pod-product-compliance
Lightning Source LLC
Chambersburg PA
CBHW070307010526
44107CB00056B/2510